TRUE SCARY CAMPING HORROR STORIES

All Rights Reserved

TABLE OF CONTENTS:

STORY 1

STORY 2

STORY 3

STORY 4

STORY 5

STORY 6

STORY 7

STORY 8

STORY 9

STORY 10

STORY 11

STORY 1

My name is Jack, and for years, I had navigated the dense, shadowy depths of the woods, honing my skills as a seasoned tracker. Little did I know that my expertise would thrust me into a world far beyond the ordinary, a world of government experiments and monstrous creatures.

Assigned by the U.S. administration, my mission was to track down a Bigfoot that had escaped from a CIA science experiment. The dense forest seemed to close in around me as I ventured deeper, an unease settling in the pit of my stomach. Hours turned to days, and my unease morphed into outright fear.

The first glimpse of the Bigfoot sent shivers down my spine. Towering and imposing, it observed me with a keen intelligence that defied the expectations of a mere experiment. I contemplated capturing it alive for the scientists, but as days passed, I realized I was outmatched.

The creature began hunting me, relentless in its pursuit through the thick woods. Outsmarting it became my only hope, yet the sinister truth unveiled itself as I delved into its origins. The scientists weren't working for the U.S. government but a clandestine organization with their own agenda.

Betrayed and caught in a deadly game, I uncovered the shocking revelation that the CIA had captured the Bigfoot, leaving me shaken. Determined to expose the organization, I dug deeper, revealing a more horrifying reality. Human DNA had been spliced with animals, creating hybrid beings released into the wild.

Driven by the urgency to prevent further harm, I found myself one step behind the scientists. A trap was set, leading to my capture and transportation to a secret facility. The experiments that followed were brutal, injecting me with substances that heightened my senses and surrounded by the growls of the hybrid creatures.

Refusing to break, I clung to the hope that someone would come for me. After what felt like an eternity, gunfire and familiar voices shattered the silence. The Just man, my fellow rescuers from the U.S. Government, had found me.

Emerging from the facility scarred but stronger, I vowed to uncover the truth and bring the scientists to justice. The horrors of the deep woods were behind me, but my true calling had just begun. I walked away, leaving the shadows behind, ready to fight against the secrets that threatened us all. The journey had changed me, but in the end, I emerged as a symbol of resilience against the darkness that lurked within the heart of the government.

STORY 2

It was a typical night, the air filled with the lingering excitement of the movie we had just watched. My boyfriend and I strolled along the familiar path towards my house, the routine of our goodbyes just around the corner. Little did I know that this night would carve a notch into my memory, etching an encounter that defied explanation.

As we reached the point where our paths usually diverged, my boyfriend and I lingered, engaged in casual conversation beneath the dim glow of streetlights. The atmosphere was serene, until an abrupt shift caught my attention. His gaze fixed on something beyond me, his expression a mix of confusion and alarm. I followed his line of sight, turning to face the unknown entity that had seized his attention.

Across a small field from us, the night played host to an enigma. A pitch-black figure, its movements reminiscent of a seal, swayed from side to side. A palpable tension hung in the air as we both observed this mysterious creature, seemingly getting closer without advancing forward. My heart quickened, a chill running down my spine as I asked my boyfriend if he perceived the same unnerving proximity. His response mirrored my fear – the creature, though motionless in space, seemed to draw near.

Our descriptions synchronized, a shared reality that left us grappling for explanations. The creature, a shadow in the night, was a source of unease and uncertainty. In the dim glow of the streetlights, we speculated about its nature, questioning the reality of what we had witnessed.

The fear lingering in the air propelled my boyfriend to offer to walk me the rest of the way home. The unknown was too close for comfort, and the eerie presence across the field left us unnerved. Together, we navigated the path towards my house, the feeling of being watched lingering until the very last step.

When my boyfriend turned to head back home, the creature had vanished. The field was once again shrouded in darkness, and no trace of the enigmatic figure remained. Questions lingered in our minds, the encounter haunting our thoughts long after the night had passed.

In the days that followed, we searched for answers. Were there others who had witnessed a similar phenomenon? Was there a logical explanation for what we had seen? Our search led us into a realm of folklore, where tales of mysterious creatures and unexplained phenomena painted a canvas of uncertainty.

Living in the UK, we delved into local legends, hoping to find a connection to the creature that had momentarily disrupted our ordinary night. Yet, as we sifted through stories and whispered accounts, the truth remained elusive.

The enigma of that night never fully dissipated, leaving us with a lingering sense of wonder and trepidation. The memory of the pitch-black creature, swaying in the night like a mysterious specter, became a shared secret between my boyfriend and me – a story etched into the tapestry of our experiences, forever unanswered and unsettling.

STORY 3

My wife and I had embarked on a journey to the Smoky Mountains from our home in Ohio, seeking the tranquility of nature for our anniversary getaway. Unlike most, we opted for the scenic and slower-paced state routes, reminiscent of the roads I traveled in my childhood. Little did we know that this trip would unfold into an unforgettable nightmare, a disaster etched in our memories.

Navigating our way with a blend of GPS and paper maps, the usual harmony in our travels gave way to confusion and frustration. Errors in our course, a rarity for us, led to an uncharacteristic argument that escalated into a heated exchange, the words flowing like disjointed languages. It was as if we were looking at different maps, interpreting the landscape through lenses of incomprehension.

As we ventured deeper into less populated and poorer road conditions in central Kentucky, the forest became hilly and expansive. Small towns and occasional farms dotted the landscape, set against the backdrop of federal land. The tension in the car eventually subsided as we anxiously followed the erratic guidance of the GPS.

Suddenly, the device chimed in with an unexpected directive: "Turn left now!" My reluctance lingered, but my wife suggested it might be an unknown shortcut. The road we turned onto, however, hinted at something more ominous. Potholes large enough to trap a tire, overgrown scrub, and ominous vines set the stage for what unfolded next.

Bringing the car to a stop, I questioned my wife about the decision. Before she could respond, she froze, staring at her phone in an unusual, almost robotic stillness. Instinctively, I slammed the car into reverse, attempting to retreat from the questionable path.

As we completed the reverse turn and shifted into drive, the rear of our Lincoln was abruptly lifted off the ground, leaving us immobilized. Before comprehension could catch up, a monstrous red blob charged from the woods to our right. Its unnatural speed and agility defied logic, moving on all fours until it stood on hind legs, its hands reaching toward the glass.

Up close, the creature's fur revealed itself to be strands of rotten flesh emitting a putrid scent of fish and moss. Its hands, almost human in appearance, sported long, menacing claws. The face, a twisted amalgamation of human and canine features, bore bloodshot yellow eyes that leered at my wife with a predatory hunger.

In a moment of clarity, I felt a primal urge to protect my mate. With a bellowed command, I stomped on the gas pedal, urging the car to escape the clutches of the grotesque creature. It scratched and banged on the car, a nightmarish pursuit that only ceased once we broke 45 miles per hour, careening wildly through the winding country roads until the lights of a town offered salvation.

We parked in a well-lit lot, our hands trembling as we inspected the car. Tearful and shaken, my wife described feeling a pressure in her head and a paralyzing consciousness during the encounter. A cracked strut and a lump of the creature's flesh dangling from the frame confirmed the reality of our nightmarish encounter.

Thoroughly shaken, we discreetly unpacked our handguns, vowing to be prepared for whatever might come next. The memory of the creature's hungry eyes and the overpowering stench lingered as we waited until the safety of daylight before cautiously resuming our journey on the highway, leaving the horrors of that night behind us.

STORY 4

As teenagers growing up in Northern Ohio, my buddy and I were always drawn to the mysteries of the night. Near Cleveland, close to Lake Erie, the woods held an allure of creepy noises and unidentified animal sounds that fueled our teenage curiosity. It was on one such night that we stumbled upon an enigma that would haunt our memories for years to come.

The moon cast eerie shadows through the trees as we ventured deeper into the woods, our senses heightened by the unfamiliar symphony of the night. That's when we noticed it – a floating, blinking blue light tracing an almost hooked J-pattern in the darkness. At first, we brushed it off as a lightning bug, but this light was different. It emitted a brilliant blue glow, almost like a high-powered LED, standing out distinctly against the backdrop of the night.

Curiosity getting the better of us, we approached the light, realizing it was only a few feet away. The absence of other lightning bugs and the uniqueness of the blue hue left us perplexed. We considered the possibility of someone with an LED light playing a prank, but the isolated location of the woods made that seem unlikely.

As we stared in amazement, the silence was shattered by an unexpected sound – a high-pitched giggle that seemed to emanate from the surroundings. It wasn't the sound of a typical prankster or a mischievous teenager hiding in the woods. The incongruity of the situation dawned on us, and a chill ran down our spines.

Without exchanging words, a shared sense of unease propelled us into action. Fear gripping us, we ran out of the woods as fast as our legs could carry us, the giggling lingering in the night air behind us.

In the aftermath of that peculiar encounter, we found ourselves pondering the mysterious blue light and its accompanying laughter. The woods, once a place of intrigue, had transformed into an unsettling realm. We shared our story with friends and family, hoping someone might provide an explanation.

Days turned into weeks, and weeks into months, but the mystery remained unsolved. No one could offer a plausible explanation for the floating blue light and the inexplicable giggle that had sent us fleeing into the night.

Years later, the memory of that peculiar night still lingers, a tale we recount with a mix of wonder and trepidation. The woods near Lake Erie hold their secrets, and that blue light, accompanied by the mysterious laughter, remains an unsolved enigma, a testament to the inexplicable mysteries that lurk in the shadows of the night.

STORY 5

Growing up in West Texas, where forests were scarce and mesquite trees dominated the landscape, my childhood unfolded in a small town of less than 2,000 people. Despite the rural setting, the city limits were well defined, and the streets remained well-lit at night, allowing neighborhood kids, my brother, and me to play until well past sundown. The tales of haunted houses and mysterious figures were part of the local lore, but nothing could prepare us for the bizarre encounter that unfolded one Sunday night in July.

Kelley, a resident known for his creepy demeanor, resided in a rundown single-wide trailer that mirrored FEMA trailers from the early '90s. Tall, with curly brown hair and thick Buddy Holly-esque glasses, he had become the subject of numerous unsettling legends in our tight-knit neighborhood. Rumors spoke of nocturnal dumpster diving, the consumption of worms, and even a disturbing incident involving a deceased kitten.

One evening, as a friend's mom claimed, Kelley had taken a kitten that had been run over and placed it down the front of his pants. The fact that the adults were complicit in these tales added an unsettling layer of credibility. Kelley's past included a mentally handicapped older brother named Bo, who mysteriously disappeared, leaving behind a static green bike under the carport that supposedly "never moved again."

Despite my propensity for spreading rumors as a child, I avoided discussing Kelley. An incident one night, playing "monster" with a friend named Alex, had instilled a genuine fear in me. As we transitioned between the backyard and the alley, Alex suddenly made a grunting, oinking noise, prompting me to dismiss it as a prank.

However, a metallic thud emanating from a nearby dumpster captured our attention. Peering into the dimly lit alley, we spotted a figure limping across the overgrown lot. The unsettling feeling of the "uncanny valley" washed over me as the figure moved with jerky, claymation-like motions. Encountering Kelley, our flashlight revealed distorted hands, a flannel shirt with teats visible, and a face resembling a pig's snout.

Paralyzed by fear, Alex and I stood there for what felt like an eternity, before Kelley emitted a bizarre half-whoop, half-squeal. We bolted, leaving the back gate open. Though my parents dismissed my account as an overactive imagination, the strange events continued. Late at night, while in the bathroom, I heard sniffing and a curious "h r m" sound outside the window, intensifying my anxiety.

Kelley became more reclusive after the encounter, and no one in our circle of friends believed our tale. One day, while he worked on his roof, Kelley sniffed the air, glanced in our direction, and hurried back inside. The question lingered: What was he? Pale with curly hair, he didn't fit the profile of a Native American. The strange speech patterns, dumpster diving, and avoidance suggested something more, perhaps akin to the lore of skinwalkers. My neighborhood, it seemed, harbored not just Kelley's secrets but a myriad of strange people with stories waiting to be unraveled.

STORY 6

I had been a park ranger for nearly a decade, patrolling the vast woods that surrounded the national park. The routine was familiar, the rhythm of nature calming, and the thrill of occasional encounters with wildlife kept the job exciting. But on this particular day, the tranquility of my routine shattered when I stumbled upon something that would change my life forever.

It started innocently enough. I was on my usual patrol route, walking along the well-trodden paths when I noticed peculiar tracks in the dirt. They were unlike anything I had seen before, neither animal nor human, and they seemed to lead deeper into the woods, towards an area strictly off-limits to the public.

Curiosity mingled with a growing sense of unease as I followed those mysterious tracks. The forest, once filled with the sounds of chirping birds and rustling leaves, grew eerily silent. The air seemed charged with an unspoken tension, and I couldn't shake the feeling that unseen eyes were watching my every move.

Hours passed, and the tracks led me to an unexpected clearing. In the heart of it stood an abandoned building, a relic from a bygone era. It seemed untouched by human hands for years, forgotten by time. As I cautiously approached the dilapidated structure, strange noises emanated from within, sending shivers down my spine.

With every creak of the door, I could feel the weight of the unknown pressing upon me. The interior revealed a bizarre scene—unfamiliar machinery and equipment cluttered the room. At the center lay a large, metallic cylinder adorned with cryptic symbols and markings. As I approached, the cylinder emitted an otherworldly glow, and before I could react, a powerful force knocked me back.

Dazed and disoriented, I awoke to a changed reality. Whispers echoed in my mind, and I could sense things beyond the realm of human understanding. In the ensuing days, the transformation became apparent. My senses heightened, and I began to experience a connection with the forest that went beyond the ordinary.

Then, one fateful night, I encountered the creature responsible for the enigmatic tracks. It emerged from the shadows—a humanoid figure with mottled gray skin and eyes that glowed with an unnatural light. Its razor-sharp claws and teeth hinted at the danger it posed. I tried to confront it, but the creature was swift and elusive, overpowering me and sending me crashing into the woods.

Determined to unravel the mysteries surrounding the abandoned building, I pieced together a grim truth. The government had conducted secret experiments, and I had unwittingly stumbled upon their failed creation—the creature that now haunted the woods. I knew I had to act, to protect both the forest and those who wandered within it.

Desperation led me to contact the authorities, but my pleas fell on deaf ears. They dismissed me as a madman, refusing to acknowledge the existence of the abomination now roaming the woods. Alone and isolated, I faced a relentless battle against a creature that defied the laws of nature.

Each passing day tested my resolve, but I refused to surrender. Armed with newfound abilities and a determination born from the responsibility of my discovery, I remained a lone ranger in the heart of the wilderness. The creature was my adversary, a manifestation of government experiments gone awry, and I couldn't rest until it was captured or destroyed.

The woods that once felt like a sanctuary had become a battleground, and as the struggle continued, I couldn't help but wonder how long I could endure this lonely fight against a creature that shouldn't exist—a fight that had thrust me into the depths of the unknown.

STORY 7

Two years ago, when I was 18, an inexplicable incident unfolded during our family's annual summer retreat to our camp in Dedham Ellsworth, Maine. Nestled about three hours away from our home, the camp, a log cabin overlooking a serene lake, held a lifetime of memories for me. However, that fateful night would etch an unsettling experience into my memory.

It was the dead of night, and everyone in the camp, including my two brothers and parents, had retired to bed. The only source of illumination was the porch light casting a feeble glow that barely reached beyond the porch itself. Engrossed in a late-night TV show, I was suddenly interrupted by a noise emanating from the kitchen. Realizing that the dogs needed to go outside, I took my brother's two pit bulls and my tiny affenpinscher named Alfie with me.

The ritual of releasing the dogs into the yard was routine, a nightly occurrence during our stay. This time, however, was different. The pitch-black darkness of the Maine woods enveloped everything beyond the porch light's reach, making it challenging to keep an eye on the dogs. My momentary distraction by the sight of a loon on the lake allowed the dogs to roam freely.

When I refocused my attention, I noticed the pit bulls fixated on something in the woods. Squinting into the darkness, I couldn't discern what had captured their attention. The realization struck me that Alfie was nowhere in sight. Panic set in as I called out for her, hearing only soft whimpering from the direction where the pit bulls had been looking.

Fear gnawing at me, I took tentative steps towards the sound, fearing that she might be trapped or injured. Just then, I felt movement behind me. Whirling around, I discovered Alfie right at my feet, silently accompanying me. Confused and concerned, I wondered why the pit bulls were growling and advancing, their attention still fixed on the woods.

Picking up Alfie, I began to back away slowly, trusting the instincts of the dogs who seemed to sense danger beyond my understanding. As I turned to retreat, a bone-chilling moment seized me. From the depths of the woods, a distorted voice called out Alfie's name. It sounded like an eerie mimicry of my own voice, a grotesque attempt that sent shivers down my spine. The voice wailed, and in sheer terror, I fled inside with the dogs, leaving the mysterious entity in the darkness.

Confused and shaken, I tried to make sense of the encounter. Our camp, perched on the edge of the lake, seemed isolated, with the nearest family neighbor residing at least half a mile in the opposite direction of the unsettling incident. What had called out to Alfie, distorting its voice in such a haunting manner? The mystery lingered, and the once-familiar woods of Maine now held an aura of unease that would forever alter my perception of our family retreat.

STORY 8

Between 1986 and 1989, an eerie tale unfolded in the southern outskirts of Porto Alegre, Brazil, specifically in the remote area of Lami where my uncles and cousins lived. My now-deceased uncle ran a small "boteco," a Brazilian restaurant, in this sparsely populated region dominated by pastures and century-old trees. The nearest neighbor was over a kilometer away, and life in Lami unfolded against the backdrop of a vast and quiet landscape.

Rumors circulated among the locals during that time about a colossal creature, a hybrid with the body of a man and the head of an animal, roaming the area. Whispers spoke of its attacks on both animals and people, with tales of near misses and lost livestock becoming part of the unsettling lore. My aunt, pragmatic and skeptical, dismissed these stories as mere "inventions of the people."

However, one night, her skepticism was tested in a way she could never have anticipated. Returning home on a bus with one of my cousins, the darkness of the night enveloping them, they became part of an incident that would send shivers down the spine of everyone on board.

With less than ten passengers, something massive emerged from the bushes and collided with the right side of the bus, causing the driver to lose control. The abrupt stop left the bus partially lodged in a ditch. Though there were no injuries, fear hung thick in the air. The driver, irritated and cursing, left the bus to assess the damage and call for help.

In the unsettling darkness, a strange grunt pierced the air, distinct from any animal or human sound. Panic ensued as passengers crowded near the driver's seat, anxiously awaiting his return. Minutes later, a resounding knock echoed once again, prompting a frantic rush to the other side of the bus. Cries and prayers filled the air as the vehicle was violently shaken, threatening to overturn at any moment.

Peering through the windows, passengers glimpsed a large figure outside, its features obscured by the night. Suddenly, the chaos ceased, and an unbearable stench invaded the bus, signaling the arrival of an unseen terror. My aunt, terrified, clutched her son close as the creature made its way toward the open door.

As the passengers huddled in the back, a grotesque figure entered the bus—a large, naked man with dark skin, a massive goat's head sporting enormous horns, and yellow eyes. The creature paused, huffing angrily, before retreating into the night, leaving the traumatized passengers in shock and disbelief.

Unbridled crying filled the bus until another arrived, summoned to help the stranded vehicle. The second driver, informed of the bizarre events, set out to find the missing driver. Meanwhile, the Military Brigade was activated, and ambulances, experts, and media descended upon the scene. Newspapers covered the incident for months, featuring articles and interviews with the terrified victims.

Despite search parties scouring the area for traces of the creature, no evidence was found. Theories abounded, but the mystery endured. Today, the region has transformed, becoming populated and vastly different from the time when the unexplainable events transpired. The creature that attacked the bus remains lost to history, leaving an unsettling enigma in the annals of Lami's past.

STORY 9

My name is Jack, a seasoned hunter with an insatiable thirst for the thrill of the hunt. The forest had become my second home, each expedition a quest for the next big prize. But this time, my sights were set on the ultimate trophy – a magnificent deer that had eluded me for years. The excitement coursed through my veins as I delved deeper into the heart of the wilderness.

As the sun dipped lower in the sky, casting long, ominous shadows among the towering trees, an unsettling feeling crept over me. The usual sounds of the forest—the rustling of leaves and the chattering of birds—were replaced by an oppressive silence. It was as if the very essence of the woods held its breath, watching my every move.

Determined to conquer my fears, I pressed on. However, with each passing hour, the line between reality and nightmare began to blur.

The trees seemed to morph and contort, their branches reaching out like gnarled hands, attempting to ensnare me. Eerie whispers danced through the wind, voices that echoed my name in haunting tones. My heart raced, and my once rational mind struggled to comprehend the horrors unfolding around me.

I questioned my sanity as the hallucinations intensified, wondering if the legends I'd heard whispered around campfires were true. Could the Windigo, a mythical creature of terror, truly haunt these woods? Shaking my head to dispel the encroaching terror, I stumbled forward.

Suddenly, among the twisted trees, the Windigo materialized. Its eyes burned with malevolent hunger, and its emaciated form loomed above me. But in the blink of an eye, the creature vanished into the shadows, leaving me to wonder if it had been real or just another figment of my tortured imagination.

My legs gave out, and I collapsed onto the forest floor. Darkness enveloped me, and the last sensation before unconsciousness claimed me was the chilling breath of the Windigo on the back of my neck.

When I awoke, the sun had risen, and the forest seemed reborn. The sounds of birdsong and rustling leaves filled the air, masking the horrors of the night before. Struggling to my feet, I felt an unsettling amnesia, unable to recall the details of my encounter with the mythical creature.

As I made my way back to civilization, the ordeal of the previous night felt like a distant, fading memory. Yet, an indescribable fear lingered within me. Something evil had brushed against my soul in those dark woods, and the memories remained locked away, hidden even from myself. Perhaps some mysteries were meant to be forgotten.

Returning home, my quest for the elusive deer remained unfulfilled. Something had changed within me—a lingering reminder that there are inexplicable forces in this world, forces that defy comprehension. The forest, once a place of solace and triumph, now held a darker allure, a realm where the line between reality and myth could blur, and the unknown could forever haunt the recesses of one's mind.

STORY 10

It was a crisp morning in Tuskegee, Alabama, as we embarked on our duck hunting adventure in the Tuskegee National Forest. The woods enveloped us, the scent of damp earth and the distant quacking of ducks adding to the anticipation in the air. As we strolled through the dense foliage, our steps softened by the carpet of fallen leaves, we paused for a quick rest.

Taking a moment to catch our breath, I gazed up at the towering trees, their branches stretching towards the sky. That's when I noticed it—a fleeting flash, barely registering in my peripheral vision. My curiosity piqued, but we had a destination to reach—the swamp where our duck hunting expedition would unfold.

Arriving at the swamp, our attention was immediately drawn to the left. There, on the beaver dam, something out of the ordinary caught our eyes. A tall, wide, and entirely black creature walked across the dam, moving upright on two legs. Its silhouette, against the backdrop of the swampy landscape, was both imposing and mysterious. It seemed not to acknowledge our presence, focused on its hurried journey into the depths of the woods.

Strangely, it appeared as if the creature carried a substantial object in one hand, adding an extra layer of enigma to the encounter. We exchanged glances, a silent understanding passing between us that whatever we had just witnessed was beyond our realm of understanding. The forest fell into an uneasy stillness, as if holding its breath.

Time seemed to freeze as we absorbed the sight before us. The creature moved with purpose, disappearing into the shadows of the woods. A chill ran down my spine, and the air became thick with an unspoken tension. Sensing that the hunting expedition had taken an unexpected turn, we silently agreed that it was time to call it a day.

Our footsteps echoed through the quiet woods as we retraced our path, leaving behind the mysterious swamp. The hunt had come to an abrupt end, leaving us with an eerie tale that would linger in our memories. We tried to rationalize what we had seen, questioning if our senses had played tricks on us or if the forest harbored secrets beyond our comprehension.

As we emerged from the woods into the fading daylight, Tuskegee National Forest stood serene and indifferent, its secrets hidden in the depths of the trees. We may never fully understand the tall, black creature that crossed our path that day, carrying an enigma in one hand and disappearing into the shadows. The woods held its secrets close, leaving us with a haunting uncertainty that would forever linger in the echoes of our duck hunting excursion in Tuskegee, Alabama.

STORY 11

One particular day in the swamp etched itself into my memory as the most unnerving experience I've ever had. It's one thing to see a sign warning about a predator in the area; it's another to be stalked by it all day. The predator in question was not some mythical creature but a very real and formidable force in the murky waters of the swamp – an enormous alligator.

I set out one afternoon on my small Jon boat, eager to indulge in some fishing in the heart of the swamp, particularly for Warmouth. The swamp was a familiar terrain for me, and I navigated about 3 to 4 miles to reach my favorite fishing spot. Alligators were a common sight in these waters, and over time, I'd learned to coexist with these creatures, understanding that respect goes a long way in their domain. They had grown accustomed to the presence of fishermen, and generally, as long as you respected them, they reciprocated.

The swamp's waters were tinted black by Tannic acid from the decaying leaves at the bottom, reducing visibility to mere inches. Anything visible just below the surface took on a dark amber hue. As I was reeling in a few catches, I noticed a pair of eyes floating about 50 to 60 yards back up the canal, fixed on me. A gator, I thought. No big deal. Opportunistic and sneaky, they sometimes stole stringers of fish left hanging over the side of the boat.

Continuing to fish, I leaned over the side to grab a Warmouth I'd hooked. Just as I pulled the fish out, a faint glint caught my eye about a foot below where my hand had been. The glint slowly rose, revealing two black eyes and an enormous jaw—the largest on any gator I'd ever seen in the wild.

Sliding back to the center of my small Jon boat, I felt the gator's back slide along the bottom, shifting the vessel slightly. For 10 to 15 seconds, I watched the beast before it swam out from under the boat. My estimate put it at around 12 to 13 feet, a massive specimen even by swamp standards.

What began as a momentary encounter turned into a day-long pursuit. I'd motor ahead to put some distance between us, only to feel that familiar 'bump' on the boat's bottom after stopping. The gator persisted, swimming off a few feet only to turn and stare at me. I felt outmatched, realizing that this dark, silent, toothy predator had the ability to sneak up on me anytime it pleased, getting within three feet before I'd even notice.

The unnerving realization set in – I was being followed by a creature that only waited for me to make a mistake. The intelligence and focus in those black eyes communicated my place in the food chain.

It wasn't the first time gators had followed me; I'd even been trailed by three simultaneously. Yet, none had ever made me so intimately aware that their sole intent was to drag me out of my boat and beneath the surface of that inky black water.

As I made my way back to civilization that evening, the encounter lingered, leaving me with a newfound respect for the creatures that ruled the swamp. The day had reminded me that nature, even in its familiar and seemingly tranquil spaces, held a raw power that could, at any moment, assert its dominance over the human spirit. The swamp, with its secrets and shadows, had once again proven its untamed and unpredictable nature.

www.ingramcontent.com/pod-product-compliance
Lightning Source LLC
LaVergne TN
LVHW021112071125
825255LV00008B/276